A Bouquet of Poems

– SYLVIA ARMER –

An environmentally friendly book printed and bound in England by
www.printondemand-worldwide.com

Mixed Sources
Product group from well-managed forests, and other controlled sources
www.fsc.org Cert no. TT-COC-002641
© 1996 Forest Stewardship Council

PEFC Certified
This product is from sustainably managed forests and controlled sources
www.pefc.org

This book is made entirely of chain-of-custody materials

www.fast-print.net/store.php

A BOUQUET OF POEMS

A catalogue record for this book is available from the British Library

ISBN 978-178456-038-6

First published 2014 by
FASTPRINT PUBLISHING
Peterborough, England.

CONTENTS

Snatched From the Jaws of Hell 1
A Better Day Today 2
A Gals' Night Out 3
Filthy Rotten Scum 5
Happy New Year 6
Benidorm 7
Ghost of Christmas 8
Two Pixies 10
The Nun Who Did Not Want None 12
The Christmas Tree Angel 13
The Frozen Pussy Cat 14
The Poorly Pussy Cat 15
The Writing On The Wall 16
Chloe 17
Ma To Wayward Son 18
Gertcha 20
Suicide of Heart 21
The Gallant Knight 23
Shirley Valentine 24
Three (Free) Souls 25
My Epitaph 26
Bon Matin (from the onion man) 27
The Merry Widow 28
Paradise Beauty 29
My Answering Machine 30
My Argument with Santa Claus 31
Dreamtime 33
Lady Of The Forest 34
Bray Beach County Wicklow 35
Next Christmas 36
The Young Dancer 37
Titania 38
The Closing of the Door 39

Imprints of Souls 40
Mermaid Tears 41
The Falls 42
Slim Gym 43
God's Earth 45
A Piece of Ireland 46
Once a Dame 48
Fer Pirates 'n' Cap'ns 49
The Secret 50
Santa Plight 51
Today I Saw God 52
Rainbow Prism Falls 53
The Halloween Ghost 54
My Halloween Party 56
Kettering 57
Hold On 58
The Spoken Voice 59
A Smile 60
Melanie Rosewood 61
The Wedding Vow 62
Our Childhood 63
My Pending Skydive 64
Och Aye the Noo! 65
Nineteen More to the Score 66
Romantic Memories of Love 67
Angels of Hope 68
Beyond the Distance 69
The English Rose 70
White Doves 71
Barney O'Brien 72
Bray Head 74
Hi de Hi 75
Snoopy the Lost 77
A Man From Devon 78
A Chavette's Lament 79
Is It Really Just Old Age? 80

Goodbye Friend 81
Smelly Bertha 82
The Weather 83
The Crystal Shard 84
Illusional Rainbow Faeries 85
Oh Happy Days!! 86
The Thistle and Rose 87
Reflections of The Soul 88
Un She Sez 89
Together 90
Enchanted Woodlands 91
Bird Flight Forest 92
Woodland Magic 93
New Life 94
A Poem for Mother's Day 95
English Country Garden 96
Violet Moon 97
The Old Grey Cross 98
My Sister 99
My Birthday 100
The Haunting 101
Good Day 102
Lost My Mind 103

A BOUQUET OF POEMS

Snatched From the Jaws of Hell

A little dormouse was brought in my house
By my pussy so playful you see,
He threw in the air without any care
But his roughness was bothering me.
So I jumped out of bed and tapped on pussy's head
"Just drop it," I yelled, "Don't be cruel!!"
My pussy just glared while I stood and stared
And the rest had me feeling a fool.
This tiny wee mouse was chased round my house
By a pussy determined to get;
I followed their tail and started to wail
As another big pussy we met.
I tripped up the mat because of the cat
All hell was let loose in that room;
Water it came from a vase falling down
And felt certain poor mouse faced his doom.
Then as I got up that mouse had some luck
He had hidden and nestled in hand;
I got into bed stroking his head
Hoping he might understand.
He got over his shock as he quietly sat
In the warmth of the palm of my hand;
He then gave a leap as my pussy did sleep
His escape he had so clearly planned.
He then got away into lightness of day
At the door he did go for the light;
I will always remember that dear little mouse
As he fought and kept up the good fight.
As he ventured outside I felt so full of pride
So tiny I wanted to cry;
I swore that dear mouse as he left the house
Turned back and then whispered goodbye.

A Better Day Today

****

Yesterday was once today
Tomorrow will follow on,
It's now today not tomorrow
But pretty soon that will be gone.
The days turn to weeks
The weeks to months,
And months they turn to years;
Let's enjoy our time of living
While we are all still here.

The Gals' Night Out

The Gals at Silvie's Facebook
Went out to have a meet;
The night was passing beautiful
As the ring was made complete.
They chuckled oh so merrily
They laughed until they dropped;
Their laughter rang around the town
And it never bloody stopped.
The cops were called and set the scene
Five drunks were taken in;
The women swore at the coppers
And said, "Our patience is wearing thin!
"Just let us girls have some fun
And please leave us alone!
"Go out and chase the robbers
'cos we ain't going home!"
The coppers looked and thought awhile
While scratching at their head;
"We'll let you female rebels go
If you promise to go home to bed!!!"
"Not on your Nelly!!!!" Wendy said
"What do you take us for?!"
And up stepped Nina with smile on face
As she sauntered through the door.
"What 'ave we 'ere"?!!" the copper said
As she was dressed in feather boa;
Said Christina on a cheerful note
"Do you wanna see some more?"
In walks Shenine with devil look
Dressed in soft black leather,
With long black boots and menacing whip;
You could have knocked 'em over with a feather.

And Sylvie laughed to see their face
And couldn't hold it any more.
She had to let her drawers down
And she p***** upon the floor.
Such hearty fun the ladies had
That they all fell in a heap;
In the place where all the coppers were
They all fell fast asleep.
So quietness dawned for just a while
And peace fell on the men,
Until the cock was crowing
Then they all started up again.

Filthy Rotten Scum

Dirty Filthy Scumbags

~~~~~~~~~~~~~~~~~~

Light-fingered bastards out on the prowl,
Give them what for, don't throw in the towel.
No one will help you and the system is weak;
They are all laughing at us right now as we speak.
Judges and police they don't care a jot,
And we have to live with it whether we like it or not.
We live amongst thieves and corruption's the game,
Since EU ruled over us it ain't been the same.
So just be aware and lock windows and doors,
And don't give scumbags the chance to steal yours.
If you do all and with everything said,
Just pull out a gun and shoot the scum dead.

~~~~~~~~~~~~~~~~~~

Happy New Year

A Happy New Year
****

The church bells will be ringing
On the eve of New Year's Day,
To welcome in the new one...
While the old one moves away.
As we toast the year with gladness
Hoping better luck will bring,
I wish you all in my world
A better song to sing.
May luck be in your pocket
May joy be at your door,
May all your children flourish
And never will be poor.
May your purse be filled with money
And your pantry full to brim;
May warmth always surround you
As the brand-new year comes in.
As I send you New Year greetings
With a toast I raise my glass;
Take Care, Stay Safe, DONT DRINK AND DRIVE!!
As the old year comes to pass.

Benidorm

~~~~~~~~~~

Hey Madge my friend in Benidorm
I'm really in the pink;
I got my suitcase packed and zipped
Except for the kitchen sink.
I really am excited, the time is rolling on
For me to come to Benidorm,
Really won't be long.
We can sing in KARAOKE
Just like we did before;
The crowds they clapped and cheered us
And gave upstanding roar.
Janice wet her breeches
When I slipped in the pool,
I really had the giggles
As I felt such a fool.
Remember that Spanish waiter
Who I was eyeing to the brim?
If I had been 20 years younger
No one else would have got a look-in.
I will save it till I get there and
Such fun we have in store,
I am off to sunny Benidorm -
Who could ask for anything more?

~~~~~~~~~~

Ghost of Christmas

~~~~~~~~~

The silence falls on haunted halls
And the walkway deathly cold;
Up comes a ringing bell
That sounds death's knell
For the story to be told.
With clanking chains
And sounds insane
A curdling scream is heard,
And the after cry as a bat flies by
Then silence, quiet, not a word.
There lies the body of a man
That Christmas never saw
Because he was a miser
And counted his money by the score.
His life was greed and never love
His hope was only him,
That he would build his money mound
But his life was wearing thin.
His thoughts were only for himself
No love nor warmth could give,
But little did he realize
Not long was left to live.
But still he built his money mound
The passion of his life;
He was void of any children
And void of any wife.
The Christmas ghost he did appear
And put an end to all his hoarding,
He scattered all his precious coins
That he was not affording.
His heart gave out as money spread
To people all around,
~~~~~~~~~

The blow was hard, the shock was great
As he fell dead on trodden ground.
The Christmas ghost he went his way
And said: “Let this be a lesson;
“Be good and spread your money around
And accept the Christmas blessing.
“Don’t be like him who lost his life
Through greed and money too;
“Remember when you go that way
It cannot follow you.”

Two Pixies

Two Pixies

~~~~~~~~~~~

Two Pixies on a Christmas tree
Looked down and really glum,
"It's boring hanging from this branch -
It's time we had some fun."
So they climbed up to the angel
Next to the silver bell;
They proceeded with a *[Chorus]*
From the carol called NOEL.
The robin red chirped up, "Be still -
Can't you pixies see that the little
Baby Jesus is asleep beneath this tree!"
Well! They looked at one another
and gave a little smile,
"We are really gonna have some fun
For a little while!"
They started the cattle lowing
The baby did awake,
They heard three wise men shouting,
"Oh! For goodness' sake!!!"
Joseph jumped up quickly
And stepped on Mary's toes,
She yelled in shock and anger
And punched a wise man on his nose.
The wise man's nose was bleeding
And the ox was there at hand;
He lifted baby from his crib
And stole his swaddling bands.
The wise men came to worship
They came in from the east,
The donkeys brayed "We came in here
~~~~~~~~~~~

To get some blooming peace!!!!"
The baby in the manger shouted with a sob,
"Shut up!!! You blooming heathens!!!
Or I will have a word with God!!!!"
Then as peace settled around the tree
With not a single sound to hear,
The angel waved her magic wand
And wished the world peace and good will
and a very Happy New Year.

The Nun Who Did Not Want None

Old Santa's on his way again
I've swept my chimney clean;
I've sent him a much bigger sack
So he can bring my dream.
A lovely man, so good and kind
If he really does exist,
Who doesn't prop up public bars
Determined to get pi★★★d.
Who keeps his nuts in his bag
And never in his head,
And doesn't think that life revolves
Around what he gets in bed.
If I don't get this kind of man
I will hate old Santa's guts;
I will punch his bl★★★★ lights out
And kick Rudolph in the nuts.
There's more to life in many ways
And this is made so clear;
If he doesn't measure up
Then he can disappear.
Santa, are you this kind of man?
Then you can ring my bell,
If not, don't bother coming!
You can p★★★ off as well.

The Christmas Tree Angel

****

I have a little angel on my Christmas tree
She sits upon a prickly branch,
Don't look comfortable to me.
She keeps waving up her magic wand
To try her great escape,
But as she moves and sways the branch
A hole is left agape.
"I am not very happy, as each day it comes to pass,
To have a prickly fir tree a-sticking up my a**e.
"Bugger 12 Days of Christmas
I can't stick just one,
With a hundred thousand needles
A-sticking up my bum.
"Just get that naughty little gnome
And put him in my place;
That will knock that silly smirk
Right off his silly face.
"Just move to the bottom and hide me if you like;
I`m not sitting for much longer
Because I will go on strike."

The Frozen Pussy Cat

****

Cripes! The snow is falling once again
My eyes are all agog,
My little balls are frozen now
'cos in the snow I trod.
My bum fur is all frozen up
My feet are frozen too;
But can't get used to indoor box
No matter what I do.
I have warmed up with cat coffee
But nothing seems to help,
Even next door's doggy
Can't resist a little yelp!
So Mr Snowman in the sky
Please make this white stuff stop,
Or we will end up at the vets
To get our manhoods chopped.

The Poorly Pussy Cat

****

Goodbye little pussy cat
Goodbye to all your pain,
Although I tried to save you
The trying was in vain.
Too many things were happening
They sent you on your way,
To be in pussy heaven
Where you can skip and play.
I saw you playing in the yard
Chasing butterfly and bees,
Your little face a pleasure as
You tried to climb the trees.
But now you have gone to heaven
Away from this cruel day;
With other little pussy cats
Together you will play.

The Writing On The Wall

The Writing On The Wall
★★★★★★★★★★★★★★★★★★★

I face the lie that there is no god
When I see the truth in this world,
For today I learned the truth in living's hell
Lies, untruths, make no difference.
When the horror ends
Then the truth lives only in that last second,
We are alone!
With open eyes I read of truth
And tears fall in cascades of splintered love.
Innocence smashed and cold
In the taking of young buds to death's vale.
Where is the light now?
"Lost"....never there, taken so quickly and cruelly,
While dying flowers all around
Cling on to their last breath.
God! I hate thee with a vengeance;
Why pretend you are there
When all around is so cruel and lost?
What purpose do we serve in this realm of cruelty?
Truth is that this is truly hell here on earth!!!

Chloe

Chloe

★★★★★★★

Soft pink petals of roses
Fall around Chloe,
Delicate fragrance
Velvet to touch.
Fragrant and uplifting
In the spirit of love,
That flows all around
An aura of purity.
Sunbeams reflect
The light of truth,
Honesty stands in hope
As love comes tapping
On Chloe's door.

Ma To Wayward Son

****

I really think you're brave, son
Living on the streets,
With tramps and druggy vagabonds
Stealing boots from off ya feet.
And pinching bag from under head
It really is a shame,
But you chose to wander far and wide
Only got ya self to blame.
I bet ya head's all clogged with lice
And you smell just like a skunk;
You beg just like a hungry dog
And your head is always drunk.
So if the Sally Army has offered you a bed
I think tomorrow morning
They gonna wake up dead.
Ya feet are caked with dead skin
'cos you suffer athlete's foot;
And still ya chew your toenails
And ya teeth are black like soot.
And ya clothes are from the ragbag
That the people all discard;
And yes, the life that you are living
Must be very hard.
Just get off in the shower and wash ya body down,
And get rid of all those nits and things
Or your mates won't stay around.
They don't wanna cage a polecat that stinks of body grime,
And I am glad you have chose the high life -
Rather yours than mine!
So I'm glad you're feeling happy
At the life that you have chose;
I bet you're muggin' old folk

To keep living, I suppose.
But goodbye son, I say to you
Don't forget to peel ya feet;
My home is so much fresher now
That you live on the street.

Gertcha

Gertcha!!!

~~~~~

Gerrof!! me ass ya mutt
And please leave me alone!
Or you won't get that present
And that lovely juicy bone.
Now me legs are all a-quiver
And I can hardly stand;
Gerrof!! me blooming trousers!!!
Afore you feel me hand!!
I saw one eye was open
As I slipped into the room,
As I came down that narrow chimney
And me belly it went boom.
Been feasting on too many goodies
And me eyes were all agog,
And I disturbed this angry fellow
That you all would call a dog.
Gerrof me ass!!! ya mutt!!!
Your teeth give out some bite;
I pulled and pulled but wouldn't let go,
So I yelled with all me might.
Gerrof! me ass, you hurtin'!!!!!
(Go and chase the cat)!!!
It dug its teeth much deeper
And everything went weird;
I escaped him all so suddenly
But I left without me beard!!!
~~~~~

Suicide of Heart

★★★★★★★★★★★★★

Caress the pain of aching heart

That softens against you,

The hurt of Mars possesses

All the planets of my soul.

Dreams fall into cascades of ice crystals

Sharp as needles, blue of colour,

Drained of red rose passion

Into an abyss

Of forever solitude.

No Moon 0

No Stars★★★

No Sun)

★falling★

★down★

twisting

★( )

turning

()*

(*)

down(

down)

into

stillness.

The Gallant Knight

★★★★★★★

The mighty sword of bravery won
A gallant knight you have become,
Though something missing found I fear
That maiden fair cut off your ear.
It's 'ear today and gone tomorrow
You were knighted with so much sorrow,
Arise my knight and don't you fret
You haven't heard the news of yet.
When fighting foe you did your best
For Lady Jane you did pass the test,
But jealousy burned in Mary's heart
A conspiracy you were a part.
Your ear is there on end of sword
While jesters in the court applaud,
A point for them in court, I fear
While jesters shouting, "'ere!, ear! Here!"

Shirley Valentine

Shirley Valentine
★★★★★★★★★★★★★

You stepped into your dream of paradise
When your thoughts took you away,
To the land of many sunsets
Where the sky is never grey.
Where the golden sky meets the sea
And the sun is burnished gold;
And your dreams were building higher
Of more promises untold.
You found the lover of your dreams
Your life was at its peak;
You really couldn't believe your luck
You found it hard to speak.
Then after a while you woke up
And found you were in your bed;
And your bald-headed ratbag
Had taken his place instead.
He got up and put his teeth in
And his toupee on his head,
Then screwed his wooden leg on
That he kept under the bed.
Put his rubber nose on
Replaced his glass eye too,
And said "I dreamed of Shirley Valentine
And woke up to you."

Three (Free) Souls

Three (free) Souls

★★★★★★★★★★★★★★★

As I stood upon the ragged rock
Just gazing out to sea,
Pounding waves beneath my feet
I am thinking but of thee.
Are you out there in the void
With seagulls flying free
Where stars are shining in the night -
Please send a sign to me.
"Where did you go?" I asked myself
My question goes unheard,
Then a salty spray upon my face
And the presence of a bird.
A seagull resting, so I thought
But No! It was a dove,
It was followed by another
That came down from up above.
They circled round above my head
And settled at my feet,
Then gently fluttered to my face
And kissed me on the cheek.
A young one flew beside them
Gave me quite a start,
And settled on my outstretched arm
And nuzzled to my heart.
My question had been answered
As the raging sea did calm,
As I stood upon the ragged rock
With three doves upon my arm.

My Epitaph

My Epitaph

★★★★★★★★★★

Although I lie beneath the ground
I am not really dead,
I am that little birdie
Flying freely overhead.
If in life you have helped me
I thank you in reserve,
If not, look heaven upwards
And get what you deserve.

★

★

★

★

★

★

Splat!

Bon Matin (from the onion man)

Bon Matin

★★

Pardon, Madam, here I am
What happened to the bar?
I am inclined to drink red wine
Please tell me who you are.
I've sold all my onions
Now have great big bunions,
And I also suffer from gout
I need therapy to set me free
So I have come for a scream and a shout.
No one is in - where do I begin?
The doors are locked up tight,
No times on the door, not been here before
Think I'll come back here later tonight.
I've gone all aquiver because my bike's in the river
And the yobbo culture is thick,
I need therapy so give some to me
Of this life I am getting quite sick.

The Merry Widow

I lay awake on Christmas Eve
And I heard this funny noise,
Falling, scratching, scuffling
Against the chimney walls.
I jumped up very quickly
Crept down the creaking stair;
I saw two legs a-dangling
From the chimney over there.
I heard this very muffled voice shout
"Please help me out of here!!!
I think I've had too much to eat
Like mince pies, cake and beer!!!"
I tugged and tugged with all my strength
I PULLED! with all my might,
Then a fat man hit the hearth
And gave me quite a fright.
He thanked me with a jolly laugh
And went merrily on his way;
I couldn't seem to place his face
Not even to this day.
He wore red clothes beneath black soot
And it really was a shame,
I did not get to ask this man -
What was his blinkin' name?!!!

Paradise Beauty

Dreamland Paradise

★★★★★★★★★★★★★★★★★

Sun warmth glow that kisses skin
A paradise to relish in;
Coconut palms that stretch to sky
Such wonder to the human eye.
Seagulls singing on the breeze
Starlight down between the trees.
Shingles echo on the shore
Who would ask for anything more?
Blue lagoon "Oh so nice."
This is a dreamland paradise.

My Answering Machine

Thank you for your telephone call
I'm sorry I'm not in,
I've gone down to Birmingham
To collect my lottery win.
And if it's my money you are after
On that I'll have to pass,
You can stick your head
Between your legs
And whistle UP YOUR A★★!!!!!

My Argument with Santa Claus

HEY SANTA
Hey Santa, where's me present
You promised I would get?
I have waited all so patiently
But haven't got it yet.
I awoke on Christmas morning
To see my stocking hanging there,
With just an apple and an orange
NOW DO YOU REALLY THINK THAT'S FAIR!?
★★★★★★★★★★★★★★★★★★★★★★

Hey Sylvie, just be patient
Your stockings cannot hold,
The present that you ordered
From me that was so bold.
It's gonna take much longer
I shall need a bigger sack;
How can I carry something
that is too heavy for my back?
★★★★★★★★★★★★★★★★★★★★★★

Hey Santa listen to me
If it don't get here soon,
I'm gonna kick old Rudolph up the a★★★
And send him to the moon.
So just you listen to me
And just you listen good;
If you don't send me present
You will put me in a mood.
★★★★★★★★★★★★★★★★★★★★★

Hey Sylvie, don't get cheeky
Or your present you won't get;
I have been travelling all night long
And me clothes are wringing wet.
I can't get down your chimney

And have lost the magic key;
It's getting quite amusing
Can't stop laughing - he! he! he!

★★★★★★★★★★★★★★★★★★★★

Hey Santa, just keep laughing
As you don't really hack,
I think you are being lazy
And you deserve the sack.
Forget your soddin' present
And you just disappear;
I will have to wait forever
For my present to be here.

★★★★★★★★★★★★★★★★★★★★

Hey Santa, I'm still waiting
For my present shining bright;
If you don't bring it to my house
I couldn't give a shi★★.
I have found another Santa
That will help in every way;
If you value your long-time job
Just get down and bloomin' pray.

★★★★★★★★★★★★★★★★★★★★★★★

His reindeer are much better
And much faster they will fly;
And they run on cheaper fuel
As they go around the sky.
Your transport is so out of date
And your face is hard to see;
And I will give you HO! HO! HO!
So bring it NOW! to ME!

Dreamtime

Dreamtime

★★★★★★★★★★

As thoughts drift on wisps of clouds
I think of you,
As sun arises with the dawn
I see you.
Like snow in lightness falls to ground
I reach out for you,
Like roses red in passion clasp
I hold you.
Like diamonds twinkle in the night
I possess you,
Like time it flies as if on wings,
I cling to you.
Like glinting stars are with the sky
I am a part of you,
In twilight hours of morning light
I am without you.
In stark, cold moments in my mind
I have lost you,
In morning's light and reality
I am alone.

Lady Of The Forest

★★★★★★★★★

She walks the pathway of greenwood forest
Her raven hair of silken shine,
She watches over little people
From Ireland's myths and fairy line.
Her watchful eye in calmness settles
On tiny creatures of this earth;
And lady raven of Ireland's green
A youthful beauty of Irish birth.
She cares for Ireland's mythical creatures
The fairies, goblins and leprechauns too,
To keep their reality alive and living
To bring such magic to me and you.
Don't let them die for unbelieving
Fairies bring magic to our day,
Always know in your believing
You drive the banshee far away.

Bray Beach County Wicklow

****

On the close of the day when the sun goes to sleep
I open my dreams and inside I peep,
At a golden memory a treasure I store
Of the sounding sea on shingled shore.
Where footsteps walked so long ago
Where the crashing waves lulled to and fro,
And a heart of gold of one I did know
And the memory shall linger forever.
The soft salty spray on cool breezy day
I felt the power of a greater design,
While stars shone so bright on that beautiful night
On the sand our two names we did sign.
I remember next day as we watched by the bay
As the rollers snatched names from the sand;
And you held me so near as our names disappeared
And we tightly clasped each other's hand.
As our names sailed to sea, oh how could it be?
Names together were pulled far apart,
As the rollers did break as each name did take
Took a part of each other's heart.
Was it God with his plan who wanted my man?
Just a glimpse of what was to be,
Was it his way of showing just where we were going
And our love could not ever be?
But my love has passed on and each time I hear this song
I wanna hold your hand,
(Beatles)
Brings back memories happy and sad.
But thank the Lord to this day and thank you, I pray,
For our short time my love and I had.

Next Christmas

Next Christmas
★★★★★★★★★★★★★

When December shows and Santa's here
This year he'll be on wheels,
His reindeer can't walk very far
I know just how they feel.
Old age is creeping up on them
It's time they had a break,
And younger reindeer for to vote
For Santa Claus to take.
Here is Blitzen, nearly blind
He can hardly see,
Who is helping weary Santa
To bring goodies for you and me.
So give a thought to animals
And give thanks to all reindeer,
For bringing us all presents
With Santa Claus each year.
Next year a Lamborghini
Will be parked outside your door,
Because all Santa's reindeer
Are not needed any more.
No chimneys up on rooftops
For Santa to get down;
We all have central heating
To keep us warm I've found.
He will soon be made redundant
Because we don't use open fires;
Maybe we should wish him luck
As in old age he retires.

The Young Dancer

The Young Dancer
★★★★★★★★★★★★★★★★

Applauding cheers at the end of performance
Swan Lake, *Sleeping Beauty*
and *Nutcracker Suite*,
Her "pirouettes" and "pliés"
A perfect blending
A graceful picture of art
On nimble feet.
Comedy, Tragedy, Love and Humour
Displayed with such beauty and elegant show;
"Arabesque" the pose of precise perfection,
Her gracefulness showing from head to toe.
Dance on young beauty, you express it so well
You are living your dream and your audience can tell,
Fly like a bird, you are reaching your dream
The school's finest dancer there ever has been.

Titania

Quietly sleeping and dreaming the dream
Titania in beauty on wild fairy theme;
The nymph and the cherubs are sleeping there too
Dreaming a fantasy as only fairies can do.
Whispers of wood winds echoes in breeze
As fireflies and angels are resting in trees.
The glow of sweet light that is spared for the night
Bathed in the softness of friendly moonlight,
Sweet dreams to Titania refresh for the day
And bring true all your dreams that are coming your way.

The Closing of the Door

As life's door closes once again
It's sad but nevertheless true,
And as you pull yourself together
Another opens for you.
It's the opening of another door
That you hesitate to take;
But fear not, just open gently
And another dream will make.
With old life dead and left behind
A smile awaits your dare;
And life greets you with a present
That you thought would not be there.
Just take that chance and you will see
Let sun come streaming through;
Just take that step and go with it -
A new life waits for you.

Imprints of Souls

Through the pine forest in dankness deep,
I feel lots of spirits around me keep.
They stay imprinted in the light,
To make a chain with those who might
Link up to those that, in the past,
Have left an imprint that will last.
As history passes and future calls,
They are with the wind when
Autumn falls.
As each leaf falls from the bough
A spirit drifts from past somehow
Reflection of what might have been,
Are with each spirit although not seen.
They tell of dreams of yesterday
Before they passed on their way,
To the angel realm in glory light
To leave imprints on a starry night.

Mermaid Tears

She sits on rock in fiery ocean
And sings the lullaby of the sea,
She craves tranquillity of still waters
As fishermen they hunt the free.
To take her heart of living creatures
Her brother Whale and Dolphin too,
Young seal pups away from mama
Not many left but now are few.
Her song now wailing across the water
Not light or sweet, but bitter tune;
Her heart now heavy for her kindred
As killing fields beneath the moon.
The sea adrift with blood-red waters
The hand of humans brings a tear;
They rule the sea and capture kindred
And make the oceans roar with fear.
Bless the mermaid's silent weeping
For her time will surely come,
When killing fields are sure to find her -
No more calling kindred home.

The Falls

May your eyes drink up the beauty of this scene
The crystal prism of the rainbow beam,
The showering waterfall cascading down
To the rocky stream that's all around.
The lush green leaves on the highest bough
In shades of darkness and yet, somehow,
The light of sun comes shining through
To reflect the ripples of white and blue.
Look at the tree; it stands so tall
Leaning over to protect it all,
Maybe it's a vision for us to see
That someone is watching over YOU and ME.

Slim Gym

****

6.30 am, here in the gym
To try and keep my body slim,
Avoiding cake and fatty food
I'm in an energetic mood.
Trying hard to look my best .
Giving me my youthful zest,
Muscles firm and skin so soft
I`m going to be like LARA CROFT.
These sit-ups I do they drive me mad
The worst exercise you could have,
Oh how they hurt my muscles bad -
I think with pain I shall go mad.
Then as I swing upon the rope
I tell myself I'm such a dope!
To be like LARA, you've got some hope!
Go wash your mouth out with some soap.
Then on the treadmill I will go
Walking for miles I'll have you know,
But getting nowhere, there's nowhere to go,
Don't want to put on weight, you know.
Can I really keep this going?
I'm reaping all that I am sowing,
Results are seen in many ways
Still dreaming of my LARA days.
Now as I swing upon the rope
In feather-like form I'm building hope,
A butterfly emerging in a shapely form
And a body just like when I was born.
No fat bits bulging, in wrongful places
No side-glanced looks from critical faces,
I'm getting there in fast-moving paces
It's like training to be in marathon races.

Then as I work and start to sweat
The weighing scales to step on yet;
Have I lost more weight? "You bet."
My time has come, my fate is set.
And as I step upon the scales
The room fills up with jealous wails -
"She's lost 7 pounds in that short time
And I feel glad that this body's mine.
So off I go to get a shower
Dreaming of this long-awaited hour,
I've done my bit, I fought the good fight
(I think I will have a take-away tonight)
And the battle starts all over again.

God's Earth

****

How does the world keep spinning round
Through the debris and the stone,
Passing by the many meteorites
That clip the safety zone?
What keeps the world on polar axis
As it thunders through the air,
As it passes many planets
And many black holes waiting there?
What stops us from exploding
As the speed of earth is fast,
Will we always move in safety
And can this safety last?
It is the greatest power
That holds us in his hands,
He holds us like a butterfly
While in his place he stands.
And when the time has come to pass
And lifts and saves us all,
I wonder where the earth will drop
I wonder where to fall.

A Piece of Ireland

~~~~~~~~

Oh carry me back to the memories I treasure
Where the greens were like emeralds
And the water so clean,
Where God and his angels were right there beside me
As I wallowed in wonder for what I had seen.

[Chorus]
Oh the angels there with me they showed me a heaven
More beautiful than anywhere that I'd ever been;
And the folk they did smile as they gave me a flower
The most loveliest welcome that I'd ever seen.
Well the boys were so handsome and the colleens so pretty
They would dance on the green near the river so wide,
Where I fell for Sean Murphy a dashing young man
Who wanted to marry me and make me his bride.

[Chorus]
Oh the angels there with me, etc.

★★★★★★★★★

But my mammy and daddy they did live in England
Would not let me stay on my island of dreams;
So I packed my belongings and came back to England
With a heart that was broken
At just seventeen.

[Chorus]
All the angels there with me, etc.

★★★★★★★★★

We each sent our letters and filled with sweet shamrock
We wrapped in green ribbons and sealed with a kiss,
We vowed we would always love one another
And never believed it would end up like this.
~~~~~~~~

[Chorus]
All the angels there with me, etc.
★★★★★★★★★

Now up in heaven my sweetheart is living
With the angels that gave us the time of our lives;
I pray he can hear me and smiles down from heaven
For the once young fresh-faced beauty
That was nearly his wife.
The years now have passed and still I remember
God showed us a time but no more can it be,
But I will never forget that beautiful place
In Bray, Co Wicklow, by the green Irish Sea.
My heart left behind in that place oh so lovely
Just wanted to keep me and only be mine;
I guess it was God and all of His angels
That was showing me he lived on slim borrowed time.

[Chorus]
Oh the angels there with me they showed me a heaven
More beautiful than anywhere that I'd ever been;
But the folks looked so sad as they gave me a flower
The most saddest welcome that I'd ever seen.

Once a Dame

★★★★★

Eeee lass it were a bugger
That sword she swished so near;
It nearly cut me nose off
And chopped me bloody ear.
Me legs just went to jelly
As I curtsied to the Queen;
I thought that I would wake up
From a very funny dream.
It was a very grand affair
I shook hands with the elite,
I went to talk to Charlie
And tripped on my big feet.
I rolled down steps on carpet
And landed on all fours;
Then I lost me balance
And ALL could see me draws.
Old Charlie started laughing
And Edward gave a hand,
The corgis started barking
And my legs they turned to sand.
My heart was beating faster
Oh! What an eventful day,
I stopped to pull me draws up
And couldn't wait to get away.

Fer Pirates 'n' Cap'ns

★★★★★★★★★★★★★★★★★★★★★★

Cum spritely lads, cum to this wench
And me your lusty feelings quench,
Sup thy nectar rum un' beer
Cum an' get your Jolleys 'ere.
A buxom lass in blossom be
Cum frollick in the grass with me;
You pirates bold I to thee look -
Be careful where you stick your 'ook.
My bossoms big an' firm and round
Like coconuts on trees around,
I be a virgin for too long
Like balloon, one p★r★i★c★k and then it's gone.
Who dare deflower this buxom lass
With skin so soft and shapely ass?
Such nectar sweet for you to sup
I be sharing with thee from my cup.

The Secret

****

In my life there is a door
Behind it is a dream;
Although I have walked a million miles
The key cannot be seen.
To me the key is precious
Though very hard to find,
Unless is found cannot reveal
The secret there behind.
So faithfully I tread the path
That leads me on my way,
To try to find the missing link
That drives me on each day.
I feel I have to do this
I know not why it's for,
But something strong is pulling me
To go beyond that door.

Santa Plight

~~~~~~~~~~

Now Santa is a jolly man,
On this we all agree;
But when he landed on a roof
He said, "Now let me see.
This chimney stack is smoking
And this is not allowed."
He tried to set the fire out
In a smelly, blustery cloud.
His reindeer stood there laughing
As his beard got rather black,
And he poured some liquid on it
That he recovered from his sack.
They heard a sizzle and a shout
"What do you think you're doing!?
You've gone and set my fire out!
And ashes are a-spewing!!!!?????"
Poor Santa he apologised
In coughing, spluttering cloud,
"But your chimney is a-smoking!
And this is not allowed!!!"
"Be off with you!" cried angry voice
"There are no children here!!!"
So off he went with reindeer
And in the darkness disappears.

~~~~~~~~~~

Today I Saw God

****

"I am not a believer," you hear lots of people say
But, as sure as the sun rises, I saw God's face today.
A little child of six months old
Was briefly in my time,
And a smile as beautiful as the sun
On tiny face divine.
He looked at me and was like he knew
His smile was just for me;
But he filled my day with sunshine
For all the world to see.
He touched my heart and brought me joy
As time stood still for me,
He held my gaze with gorgeous smile
And he set my spirit free.
Joe was his name, his mother said
And, as they turned to go,
I swear I caught a glimpse of God -
He came to me, I know.

Rainbow Prism Falls

As I walk through a woodland paradise
My senses drown in the beauty of this time,
All my senses are engaged in magic mind potions
That lift me to another sphere.
As I breathe in the scents of the woodland offerings
I see the sun dancing through boughs,
And branches of lush, green leaves
That sway gently on a soft, balmy breeze.
The scent of flowers rises up to meet me
Delivering me to a paradise of my past,
My ears are filled with the sounds of beautiful birds
Singing at the beauty of this day.
Hark! I hear water falling and
As I turn and twine the woodland pathway,
I see a vision of loveliness
In the form of a magic waterfall.
My eyes drink up the wonder of this beautiful sight
Glowing with colour of rainbow prism,
Sparkling, dancing, with all the colours of the rainbow
And I am in awe at it all.
Reaching out to the water I feel the delightful spray
As it falls heavily to the stream below,
This must be heaven, as only such as this
Can be so lovely.

The Halloween Ghost

The howling winds wrap round the trees,
The gusts they rock the bough;
The screammmmming!!! echo of an owl
Is calling to him now.
The village cat stands (back arched)
Its shackles rise to sky;
Then the headless village Halloween ghost
Comes on walking by.
Head under arm he makes his way
The village dog does howl,
As Godfrey the headless vampire ghost
Is outward on his prowl.
His eyes all gleaming, flashing bright
Reflection on the trees,
When Godfrey shows his vampire fangs
He will bring you to your knees.
The thunder echoes around the wild
The lightning flashes bright,
As Godfrey the headless vampire ghost
Drifts slowly through the night.
He looks to left and then to right
While searching for his prey,
To try and find a pint of blood
Before the break of day.
The village cat, it gives a shriek
As open streets aband,
While Godfrey the hungry Halloween ghost
Begins to show his fangs.
In the distance a sudden cry
An eeerie! EErie!!! sound;
And the body of a victim
Is laying on the ground.
As blood oozes from Godfrey's mouth

A look of victory so proud;
He turns and says, “GOODBYE folks
Must get back to my shroud.”

My Halloween Party

Been stirring up my cauldren
Frogs' legs and wizards' nails,
Spiders' feet and beetles' toes
And shells from quishy snails.
Tonight's our night as we all prepare
Together as we fly,
To catch all the little horrors
As up in the sky we fly.
Black cat is by our wicked sides
To help us with their claws,
To scupper in the children's house
As each opens up their doors.
Cackle! Cackle! Cackle!
Most are looking thinner,
But fat children we are looking for
To gobble up for dinner.
So Mcdonald's fans we do pursue,
They are our only wish;
They are the one and only kind
Make up our tasty dish.
Hahahahahahhaahahahaa!!!!! Cackle!

Kettering

I remember Kettering when I was young
I was only six months old;
Mum used to walk me round the gasworks
To cure me of a cold.
And Wicksteed Park as it was
And Headlands bridge I see;
That's where we spent our childhood
All my friends and me.
Then Alfred East Gallery
I spent a lot of time,
Just wishing and believing
That all those paintings could be mine.
Highfield School I claim my own
They named it after me;
I was the first one in that school
In 1953.
The man came with a camera
He made me stand and smile,
He presented me with a story book -
I kept it for a while.
The market place was good then
With stalls so many more,
With lots and lots of lovely things
And toys stacked round the floor.
Then Parish Church my senior school
No longer is around;
They knocked it down years ago
And razed it to the ground.
But memories will always be
While places pass away,
We move along to better things
To live the modern way.

Hold On

Go where your heart takes you;
Never stall or you will lose the moment.
Nothing comes to you without a reason,
Live your dreams, reach out to the magic,
Sense your feeling...s;
You only lose it if you let it go!
Hold on to the magic and keep it forever.

The Spoken Voice

The Spanish voice is beautiful
Its mysteries must be found,
To delve into and understand
The wonder of such sound.
The powers that be gave you and I
The privilege of this fate,
A chance to learn and understand
As to communicate.
So why, we ask the powers that be
Are we the chosen ones?
To have the chance to learn it all -
To speak in foreign tongues?
We are the key to unlocked doors
Of mysteries of man,
I believe the powers that be
Have for each of us a plan.
I like to think the plan for me
Is as simple as is plain -
That the powers that be
Have a plan for me
To live in a beautiful villa in Spain.

A Smile

★★★

A smile is such a sweet thing
It opens windows of the soul;
The eyes so full of loving light
The lips that make it whole.
The sunshine shown to others
As your face lights up the day,
That brings happiness to all of friends
As they go their worldly way.
So smile at all who pass you
And they can pass it on,
And light up this dark and dreary day
And add a little song.
I can smile and so can you -
Pass it on to others, too,
They can pass it to a friend
Around in circles and around the bend.
Around the corner in dark, dark places
Are sunlit heavens and happy faces,
Just smile and let you heart begin
To open windows from within.

Melanie Rosewood

★★★★★★★★★★★★

Melanie Rosewood flits on high
She flits on cornflowers blue as sky,
She reaches out to butterflies near
As Melanie Rosewood drops a tear.
Her touch is gentle while the moment holds
As she nestles on the marigolds,
The golden daffs and poppies red
While misty thoughts fly through her head.
Her time is short, a precious thing
While she listens to the songbirds sing,
Her loving heart filled with elation
Melanie Rosewood is only just (Imagination).

The Wedding Vow

******

Corner me not into being a twin of yourself
Allow me to be me, my own person, my own pathway,
Let not your way make me into another you
That cannot hold part of me.
Let mine eyes see the truth of my being
Not as a shadow that once was alive in life itself,
Allow not my soul to be destroyed
With trying to be that for which I am not.
Let us as two people be as one
But only in the love that binds our hearts and souls,
And not in the being of one's individuality
For you loved me for me, and not for what you
Hoped that I would become.
Let love itself manifest the binding of two souls
Not as a possession of each, but as a token of eternity;
For without these, love cannot flourish.

Our Childhood

As I venture back down memory lane
I always think of you,
Of sherbet lemons and humbugs
And smoking Woodbines too.
The fun we had on carefree days
Playing rounders in the street;
And pictures in the afternoon
To us was such a treat.
I see pantry doors and radios
And us hiding in a hurry;
Us singing in the living room -
Doris Day and Ruby Murray.
I hear banging on the bedroom floor
"Who have you got down there?"
I see a lively hamster
Bedding in the chair.
Little Jimmy in his cage
Just above the door;
Us singing and tap-dancing
On a shiny, linoed floor.
There was Jean and there was Nino
There was Rose and there was John;
There was Donald and his wellingtons -
Where have those young days gone?
The summers were much longer
The weather was so hot;
But still we can be thankful
For everything we've got.
Our children gave us our delights
Now they are parents too,
They made us into grandmas
Those children, me and you.

My Pending Skydive

★★★★★★★★★★★

Flying free is where to be
No strings or ties to anchor me;
Like flying eagle on eager wings
I long to fly above earthly things.
I want to feel the wind on face
To touch on heaven far from this place,
To soar like bird or gliding plane
To fall so free, like summer rain.
To feel the rush of excitement, dare
To race the winds without a care,
To know why birds forever sing -
I want to try this magic thing.

Och Aye the Noo!

~~~~~~~~~~~~~~

Och aye the noo!! It were a party
Thae farts were blowing big un' hearty,
They gang and blew aroond thae room
And Rabbie's were aw sonic boom.
Thae rooms thae shook and Sporans jumped
Because ooer Rabbie went and pumped,
Remember Laddie as ye go
Nae draws on trump-hole doon below.
Nae wunder aw thae did complain
Nae draws the Scotsman wear, no naen,
Thae Sporan's there to hold it doon
To stap it wafting roond thae room.
When neeps and totties run thae chase
Un' greetin' looks on chappies' face,
So gaen tae party of Scottish Kilts
Mak sure the flooers never wilts.
In handbag tak a mask to don
Fer whisky farts shall kill ye, mon,
And ooer the haggis in ya gut
Wiflag doon gasses oot ya butt.

~~~~~~~~~~~~~~

Nineteen More to the Score

Nineteen lives gone now
Tragic at the loss,
While families grieving
At this terrible cost.
Why, we ask
Must these things be?
The suffering and pain
For all to see.
Where are you GOD?
If you exist,
Is it a game?
Like pic 'n' mix?
To see who you
Can knock down first?
Like a game of skittles
To death from birth?
Never understand this hateful life
Full of death and pain and strife;
Why bother to be born?
Why bother at all
When we are all like skittles
And we all must fall?

Romantic Memories of Love

Thoughts of you hang like silken cobwebs
In the canyons of my mind,
Golden dreams of pearl-drop kisses
Soft sweet embers my heart entwine.
Golden starlit days of honey
Sweet nectar supped at heaven's door,
And rainbow raindrops fall from soft clouds
Cotton like candy was our store.
Pearls of wisdom, flight of fancy
Diamond rings and all such joy;
Us in love and carefree smiling
From the young, both girl and boy.
Father Time is rushing forward
Time it takes us to the end,
But always live in treasured memories
Of my sweet, devoted friend.

Angels of Hope

Smile sweet angels, bring hope all around
Tell us of things in life you have found,
Are we just dreaming of peace on the shore?
Will we be blessed with this evermore?
Is it a dream we reach out to touch?
A thought that is golden we cling to so much?
Or is it of life a reality glow
To uplift us from sadness and wrath as we go?
Send us a dream on the starlit night
Show us the way and make it all right,
Do we have hope or do we just wait?
Accept all that comes and welcome our fate?

Beyond the Distance

What lies beyond the rainbow bridge?
What magic does behold?
Of untouched pathway walked by none
What magic will unfold?
Would you care to walk this bridge with me?
Each step will light our way,
And bring us nearer to the truth
That none have known today.
I sense calm, and beauty, and so much love
And peace beyond our sphere,
As I take a step on rainbow bridge
That is void of any fear.
A light so bright it holds my gaze
A figure bathed in light,
Is this the path to heaven
That I have gathered in my sight?
Like a soaring bird my heart takes flight
And a feeling of being free,
Would you like to take a magic walk
On rainbow bridge with me?

The English Rose

~~~~~~~~~

In a Northampton village called Althorp
On an Island that is small,
Full of beautiful flowers
That was a gift from one and all.
On this lovely sacred Island
Where no-one really goes,
There blooms the most loved flower
They call the English Rose.
Although her petals are not seen
By us with human eye,
They bloom in heaven yonder
Beyond the bright blue sky.
For her heart is ever with us
Her work is ever seen,
Beneath this tiny Island
Lies Diana, our beloved Queen.
(Of hearts)

~~~~~~~~~

White Doves

~~~~~~~~

Across grey sky they spread their wings
Peace doves as pure white snow;
They spread the heavenly gospel
That people do not know.
In heaven's domain at rainbow's end
They lift the darken cloud,
And sing to all on earth below
Of Jesus in the crowd.
We cannot see him where eyes look
For he is in our hearts,
He loves us and guides us everywhere
Of us he is a part.
So fly, white doves in summer rain
And let your song be heard,
You are the precious wings of prayer
The blessed, peaceful bird.

~~~~~~~~

Barney O'Brien

Barney was an Irish man
He lived in Donegal,
He loved to have a little drink
And always had a ball.
He loved to eye the ladies
Who always had their say,
But found his poor wife, Bridie
Always got in the way.

[Chorus]
Singing hi de hi and fiddle dee dee
He was an Irish rover;
Each time he opened up the door
His wife she pulled him over.

★★★★★★★★★

Each Sunday on the same old dot
The bar door swung open wide;
And there was Barney on a stool
With a young, pretty colleen by his side.
"Now listen here," poor Bridie said
"Ya ejit, just you listen;
All our bairns are bare-footed
And food they are a-missing."

[Chorus]
Singing hi de hi and fiddle dee dee
He was an Irish rover;
Each time he opened up the door
His wife she pulled him over.

★★★★★★★★★

"Seventeen bairns they're needing fed
And they all are needing shoes,
So stop ya gallavanting

And stop filling up on booze.
"Ya dinner's in the oven
And the bairns are waiting there;
"So you can throw them all the bones
For all of them to share."

[Chorus]
Singing hi de hi and fiddle dee dee
He was an Irish rover;
Each time he opened up the door
His wife she pulled him over.

****

Well the girls they moved so very fast
They said that he was bad,
To congregate in public house
With all the bairns he had.
So they left him sitting on his stool -
The man was all alone,
He turned to all his drinking pals
And said: "I'm going home."
Alas no bairns did he possess
But his wife was there at hand,
To stop the man from straying
From off the marital land.
She made him feel so very bad
As not lower could he stoop;
But Barney knew this was not so
As he was stuck with brewer's droop.

[Chorus]
Singing hi de hi and fiddle dee dee,
He was an Irish rover;
Each time he opened up the door
His wife she pulled him over.

Bray Head

In Eire's Co Wicklow
In the year of '62,
I scaled the sugar mountain (Bray Head)
And have beautiful memories, too.
A cross at top I wrote my name
Engraved it oh so deep,
That winds and sun cannot destroy
Forever there to keep.
I smile as I remember
How the beautiful Irish Sea,
Mingled with the shades of green
As the sun shone down on me.
As I stood in awe at beauty
That I've never seen again,
I wish I was back in Wicklow
Just sweet sixteen back then.

Hi de Hi

★★★★★★

Good morning campers, it is me
I hope your day is trouble-free,
And, as you tread the magic path
I hope you're all up for a laugh.
It makes a difference if you smile
Instead of being miserable all the while;
Your toast is ready and cornflakes too
And lots more goodies there for you.
And as you leave your holiday chalet
Be careful when you step in alley,
'cos toilet's blocked and overflowed
And stink is running in overload.
Be careful where you step on path
That you don't slip upon your arse,
We have tried our best to clear it up
But so far don't seem to have much luck.
And as you sit down to eat
3 inches of water will surround your feet,
Your shoes will smell but what the heck?
Just be thankful it's not up to your neck.
I apologise by the way -
There's NO hot water here today,
There's plenty of water here for free -
Go take a bath in our lovely sea.
And Gladys is not very well
She is lovesick, I can tell,
She doesn't know just where she's going
Always passing, to-ing and fro-ing.
And Gerald, well, he is such a dope
On him I have given up hope,
He only climbed up the ladder
Can you think of anything sadder?

He said he went to rescue cat
He then fell and landed on his back,
Although it gave campers laugh
It now has left us short of staff.
So no beds made within your chalet
So all around us will have to rally,
To make this holiday a success
Even though things are such a mess.
So I bid thee all a sweet farewell
An amazing holiday I can tell,
And, as I quickly disappear
I hope you all come back next year.
HI DE HI, CAMPERS!

Snoopy the Lost

Calling Snoopy, so slinky, and graceful
That walks the miles that are lost,
Searching for home of the love he has come from
Through unknown paths of uncertainty and loneliness.
Was it a feline lady that led you away
From the caring love of those that adopted you?
That yearn to feel your soft body of fur
And the comfort of the happy purrrr!
That you trusted them enough to give?
They loved you, and healed you,
From the wrath of humankind
That abused you and treated you badly.
Your tail is half gone and your face is not as it was
But, to those that love you, you are beautiful,
They cry for you, and they are lost without you
Slinky and black cat, turn around and walk the other way
And come home.

The Man From Devon

****

There was an old man from Devon
Who lived to be one hundred and seven,
Although he was dead inside his head
He was determined to get into heaven.
So at heaven's gates he rang the bell
And St Peter said, "You Go To Hell!!
It's warmer down there
And two horns you will share,
And stolen goods you will be able to sell."
So the old man took up earthly wares
And siddled down ten flight of stairs,
He said, "COR THIS IS HOT!!!!
WHAT A TERRIBLE SPOT;
ALL THIS HEAT IS SINJIN' ME HAIRS!!!!"
He tried to hang on to his beard
It got hotter then just disappeared,
His face went all stale
He started growing a tail
And his ending was so very weird.

A Chavette's Lament

Oh to nok a coppa's blok
I wud luv to nok a coppa off,
To nok a coppa's blok
To bang da dude up on da wall
An' gag 'im wiv a sok.
Den get da cake ass up da wall
An' bevel til ee dun,
An' get 'im beg fer meurto
An' see da coppa run.
Dem blu ass flies 'no' nuttin'
Dey dig dey dig fer shit,
Dey clam up mud fom zzzedland
An' mek da story fit.
Da coppa ain't a coppa
Da dude ain't pass no test,
Till dey 'as trapped a good man
An' robbed 'im of 'is best.
Innit! Bro!

Is It Really Just Old Age?

~~~~~~~~~

Now Ladies and Gents, please take a seat
And listen here to me;
Have you ever lost your glasses
And your flippin' front door key?
Have you ever put something away
To hide it for safe keepin'?
And buggered as where you put it
And everywhere ya peepin'?
You turn the house all upside down
And you do a merry dance,
You walk for miles around the place
As from here to bloomin' France.
And ya stop ta put the kettle on
Because you're breaking into sigh;
Then you turn for just a minute
And bloody thing's boiled dry.
Have ya ever made a Yorkshire pudding
And put it in to cook?
But can't smell the sweet aroma
So you go to have a look?
You find it in the freezer
Accompanied by your purse,
Then you are really getting senile
And we all must think the worst.
Please don't tell the doctor
Just carry on each day;
Because as sure as we are sitting here
We will all be dragged away.
We gotta stick together
And musn't fly in rage,
It really is just natural -
It's really just old age.
~~~~~~~~~

Goodbye Friend

****

Just got the news of your departing
Weighing me down like a stone on feather,
A so good heart that cared for my sorrows
And genuine in your kindness and love.
That taught me that the world still held
Light and love, kindness without greed,
After all these years a candle burned still
Within our hearts, and the world was unaware.
Thank you my love, I will always treasure our
Moments in time and the world will be a sadder
Place without you. Will miss you muchly.

Smelly Bertha

Ee our Bertha is a luverly lass
And she is princess of 't' day;
But when she gets up in 't' morning
She blows us all away.
It rather is quite funny
And we al'as laffin' still,
But the smell it drives us crackers
Like a pig come art o' swill.
We stick noses darn our jumpers
And the fan is wafting round,
But it all's jus' keeps a movin'
Round, and, round, and round.
She needs a dose of liver salts
To clear 'er system art,
But 'ope she tells 't' family
So's we are not abart.
Eee up she's a-coming
And 'er belly's big and round;
Cor 't' smell is art o' order
And 't' pong is quite profound.
She smells wus' than a polecat
And a pig wi'out a snart;
It's time wi got our Bertha
An' chucked 't' bugger art.

The Weather

Whatever the weather
And whether it's not,
Be raining or shining
Or doing the lot.
Whatever the weather
And whether it's dry,
We must weather the weather
Until we die.

The Crystal Shard

Glowing aura of colour hues
Reflecting out in pink and blues,
Greens and purples, reds and gold
From mythical crystal shard of old.
Powers of life glow from within
From gelfin child to the race of Gen,
To break the spell by prism white
From outward show of glinting light.
The treasure sought and found in deep
While in the earth the Gen they sleep,
Take up the stone and hold up high
Let sun reflect from dreaming sky.
To bring to gelfin freedom home
The crystal shard...their wishing-stone.

Illusional Rainbow Faeries

~~~~~~~~

I have been to Ireland
And Leprechauns I have met,
Along with little people
Who I will not forget.
And faeries decked in wonder
With great transparent wings;
But now you try to tell me
They are not real, these things?
The faery queen is beautiful
She slides down to rainbow's end,
In tow with lots of little ones
And they are all her friends.
The rainbow is their treasure
And I can tell it's real,
I can tell you honestly
Their colours I can feel.
I reach out hands to touch them
Inside they send a glow,
The colours are so vibrant
And are so very real, you know.
So leave me here in wonderland
The place I prefer to be,
Don't take me back to illusion
Because that's just reality.

~~~~~~~~

Oh Happy Days!!

The News
I awoke this morning
With joy beyond compare;
I listened when you told me
And was so glad that you were there.
Your words were magic to my mind
Like jewels in a crown,
I accepted the words you gave me
And I would never let you down.
You placed a smile upon my lips
Such news that I will treasure,
They made me feel so good inside
And will forever and ever.
And when it comes I shall see the time
That miracle I will see;
And we will bond forever
As a happy family.
Thank you!

The Thistle and Rose

****

It started out exciting
Like the buds that burst in bloom,
And your eyes stood out like hat pegs
As I walked into a room.
Your pulse, you said, beat faster
As the garden of love saw day;
But all too soon my sweet, sweet, love
The weeds got in the way.
You choked my life with possessiveness
And jealousy did abound,
And, like the brambles of a blackberry
You pierced my heart, I found.
You saw the ending of my bloom
A rose that stood so strong,
So I threw you on the compost heap -
The place where you belong.
This wilted Rose shall rise again
And will avoid another thistle;
Will listen to the gentle wind
As to my petals whistle.
To send my seed to garden new
Where I shall spend my hours,
With love with me for company
Sorting weeds out from the flowers.
So as I take my rightful place
With my new love by my side,
I shall look back and will remember
That old thistle that withered and died.

Reflections of The Soul

~~~~~~~~~~

What is this place that I have reflected upon
That leaves me not quite touching a full
Consciousness of this memory?
As I walk through near darkness, content and
At peace with myself,
I glance and feel
The scents of my spirits past.
Rain is falling outside,
And always I feel joy
Of the falling raindrops,
And I am always at peace.
The scent of sandalwood rises to meet me
And the dream-catchers
That catch my searching eye
Send me a feeling of past times.
Beautiful music of harps and angels' voices
Fill me with pure peace.
Candles and sweet-smelling oils fill the air
With sweetness of past times.
Soft silence in treading these past blooms
Find in me a tinkling of wind chimes.
Faeries in woodland stand before me
To dance the dance of hope;
And crystals in colourful hue
Give out a magic at a glance
And I feel a prayer from my soul
Unto heaven.
Blessed be this place that I have discovered,
For I have found my way home.
~~~~~~~~~~

Un She Sez

The Lokal Noos

★★★★★★★★★★★★

'Ere air Kate air Jack is ded;
'Ee fell an' landed on 'is 'ed.
An' gawd yew shud of seen 'is face -
Not fit to be in 'ooman race.
Air Nellie's gon un' took a turn;
She slipped an' fell on slimey wurm.
Un' 'arold's gon an' slipped a disc;
Thay say 'is life is stiw at risk.
Not many friends R left but feu -
Wot is this wurld a-cummin' to?
When gooin' private iz the gayme
The NHS wun't be the same.
Oi've lived me loif, oi've dun me best,
Und pretty soon will be at rest.
No trip to moon up in a rokit,
'cos guvermunt's robbed us in the poket.

Together

May the pathways of life that you tread
Be paved with gold and decked with the
Fragrant petals of a million fresh roses.
May the rain that falls into your lives
Be just a shower to revive and replenish
The sweetest rose that keeps the love
Blooming through all of your married life.
May any tears that you cry be tears of
Happiness, sealed with the crystal clarity
Of your love for one another,
And may the bond and meaning of your rings
Be like the rainbow in all its glory,
Saying to the world, "I am" and "You are
Part of the universe; we are as one, forever."

Enchanted Woodlands

★★★★★★★★★★★

Dog roses bloom on tangled branches
While woodbine hangs on sylph-like stems,
Fragrance in the air of bluebells
Violets and primroses as pathway bends.
Around the pathway was childhood magic
Told in fantasy and wondrous tales,
Is the fairy of spring and summer
As the light of daylight pales.
The darkness holds the scent of night stox
And dampness holds the toadstool well,
As more deep fantasy of our childhood
Visions of fairies in the dell.
Hold tight your dreams you maidens ageing
Let your childhood smile down today;
For only once shall we remember
Our childhood days that passed this way.

Bird Flight Forest

Sheltering from the sunlight
A little tiny bird,
Is posing for a photograph
For someone special, I have heard.
He sits and sings so beautiful
For him, for you, for me;
It's "Tweet, tweet, tweet,
Warble," as he sits upon his tree.
His little wings so downy
As he flutters off the rain,
He said, "I like attention -
Must come back here again."
So he sits awhile in sunlight
With rainbow way up high,
Then flies back to his mother
Who is looking from the sky.

Woodland Magic

~~~~~~~~~~~~~

Dancing on droplets of forest rain
In wonderland of enchantment fair,
Winged fairies in the dusk of dawn
Bring magic to the woodland air.
Quietly in vision bright as diamond
The glinting quest of morning sun,
Brings forth the closing of the darkness
As golden magic is lightly spun.
Without a care she weaves her magic
On mossy falls of silken palm,
To show the magic of the dreamland
That's cast in tranquillity calm.
The fantasy is alive and dancing
In woodland shades of evergreen,
As she settles and she slumbers
In reality's hardened dream.

~~~~~~~~~~~~~

New Life

Bloom forth the yellow of colourful spring
Your beauty petals glow,
From cold rough winds and chilly gales
Through bitter ice and snow.
Born new life in springtime rain
So shall we be born again,
As we rise in resurrection
To the risen Lord "Amen".
All life things must pass away
It's the order of the earth,
Like the dying of our precious Lord
Who came through holy birth.
As winter takes the dying flower
All withered to decay,
Is born again to springtime
To face a brand-new day.

A Poem for Mother's Day

****

A mother is a precious thing -
She gave you your own life;
So do not turn your back on her
Now you have found a wife.
Take care of her and respect her
Lavish her with care,
You will turn away a little while
And will find that she's not there.
So if you have wandered from her
As time and tide has changed,
A little note of gratitude
Can turn another page.
Pick up that phone and talk to her
Make this her special day,
Let differences and grudges
Just disintegrate today.
A mother is your life-line
And her tears they break your heart;
So just look back and remember
How it was, right at the start.

English Country Garden

The archway stands so big and tall
While honeysuckles abundant fall,
To meet the roses in full bloom
And lavender gives sweet perfume.
Michaelmas daisies, Lady's Smocks
Love-in-a-Mist and hollyhocks,
Gillivers and London Pride
While violets in the garden hide.
Lilies floating on gentle breeze
Japanese Cherry, my favourite trees,
Apple, plum and blackberry too
Majestic magnolia there are just two.
Gardenia flower scent fills the air
Orange blossoms beyond compare,
Wonderful blooms that were on show
But now are gone - where did they go?

Violet Moon

~~~~~~

Intense sky decked with soft stars
Like diamonds on soft black velvet,
Shining down to Mother Earth
Whose friendly ocean is her constant companion.
As she shimmers in the moonlight
Soft waves caress her,
Shifting sands sing lullabies of dreamtime
As she quietly watches on.
Palms sway in splendour to cool her
And shade her from heat,
As she gazes at the lonely lighthouse
That lights them all.
Is this just chance that beauty, light, compassion
And love can gather together in one?
Or is it part of a living pulse that beats for life
And all living things?

~~~~~~

The Old Grey Cross

I wandered across the old ragged hills
And the sky met the sea on my way,
As I looked to the clouds at the top of the hill
There stood a cross that was concrete grey.
I was led to this cross that was still in the earth
As it stood looking over the sea,
I climbed to this cross at the top of hill
And it painted old Ireland for me.
All the colours it gave that was only of green
Every shade that was born for to see;
There were 40 to witness and with beauty did show
That only Ireland could conjure for me.

My Sister

~~~~~

When the springtime warmth fills the air
And the daffodils are in bloom,
With the cheerful voice of a blackbird's song
And a sound of a familiar tune.
The scent of the garden comes alive
Brings a memory to my mind;
I think of you, my sister
As we move through space and time.
A single falling leaf in autumn
As it flutters to the ground;
I ask, "Is that you, my sister?"
I can feel you all around.
Music playing in the distance
Of a song you loved so dear,
I know that's you my sister
Telling me that you're still here.
When a snowflake settles on my face
As the snow it starts to fall,
On a gentle breeze in winter
I can almost hear you call.
When the summer rose comes into bloom
And the perfume fills the air,
That's when I see you clearly
And know that you're always there.

~~~~~

My Birthday

Today is my birthday
Oh my! I do feel old,
Where did all those years go
So many memories to unfold.
It don't seem five minutes
I was playing in the sand,
Building dreams like sand castles
For a future here to stand.
The years slip by so quickly
No time to stop and stare,
I have to grab the next fence
In my life that's waiting there.
I hope it is exciting
I need adrenalin rush,
I really should step on the edge
While someone gives a push.

The Haunting

****

A solitary castle in gloomy forest
Quiet and eerie in misty form,
Who lives within the castle walls
In dank, dark forest, wet and warm?
Is it noble? Or is it evil?
Perhaps Count Dracula with his clan?
Or maybe knights who are so noble;
Is it beast? Or is it man?
As night creeps in a sound unusual -
Bats or screams of tortured fright,
Bringing eerie feels of tension
To this creepy, dark of night.
Maiden weeping in the distance
Ghostly shadows shade the trees;
Frightening laughter fills the air
While life around all starts to freeze.
Eeeeeeeeooooow - the sound gets louder
Tortured cries through time are heard,
Is it sounds of tortured humans?
Or is it sounds from forest bird?
Sleep and rest in your slumbers
Forget the sounds you hear of fright,
Is it beast or is it man that haunts this castle
day and night?

Good Day

May your day be filled with gladness
May the sun always shine for you,
May the blackbird sing his merry tune
And God be watching over you.
May your heart be beating gladly
As it greets a brand-new day;
And may moments that you spend with friends
Just chase the blues away.

Lost my Mind

****

I always can't remember
'cos it's easy to forget,
Where I put my memory
I haven't found it yet.
I keep going round in circles
To see if I can find,
Why I can't bring it with me
And is always left behind.
I search and search to find it
In nooks and crannies, too,
But just wonder where I left it
I can't tell - can you?
I thought I left it up the stairs
But maybe not, I fear,
'cos when I go and look for it
I swear it's still down here.

ND - #0259 - 080726 - C0 - 216/138/9 - PB - 9781784560386 - Gloss Lamination